Walking On The Beach In A Girdle & High Heeled Boots

By

J Ann

Printed in the United States of America

First Edition, 2022
PAPERBACK ISBN 979-8-218-03146-6
EBOOK ISBN 979-8-218-03147-3

Red Pen Edits and Consulting, LLC
P. O. Box 25283
Columbia, SC 29223
www.redpeneditsllc.com

Note To Self

I am grateful to be able to actually hear and feel the change happening on the inside of me. I hear it in how much more often I offer forgiveness to myself and others. I feel it in the authentic love that overwhelms me as I share spaces with individuals with whom I just met.

Table of Contents

Preface

In the middle of a cold winter day, after a very difficult moment of being enthralled in the mire of a parental crisis: fighting for my son's rights at school while simultaneously using the moment as a teaching moment...I was sinking fast! Somehow, some way, I mustered up enough fortitude to exercise my freedom to stay on top. On that cold winter day, I drove from the place of crisis, 40 minutes away, to the beach: Water, the place where I feel the most freedom. That 40-minute drive felt as if I was driving 3 days to the West coast. Finally, I made it! I rolled out of my vehicle, shuffled toward the sounds of the waves crashing against each other and the smell of the salty water until my eyes met the pale sand that stretched for miles. I emerged onto that sandy seashore in a skintight girdle and four and one half inch high heeled in boots. WAIT, WAIT, WAIT, before you complete that visual in your head, I was NOT naked in a girdle and high heeled boots. I was fully clothed dressed for the winter season. There was no time to consider changing from my present attire to more appropriate clothing for a walk on the beach: I HAD TO DO SOMETHING QUICK, FAST AND IN A HURRY! I needed to respond in a way that would jolt me from being buried in my present crisis to a posture and position to embrace and believe that I will NOT die here! The more I walked, the more the girdle seemed to be closing in on me; pressing in tighter and tighter while my boot heels dug deeper and deeper in the sand, grabbing shells and seaweed with each sink. In that very difficult moment, I walked on the beach in a girdle and high heeled boots until I cried, shouted, and prayed, releasing frustration and anger to embrace peace.

Like most of you, I've had to face some very difficult and tumultuous seasons in my life. My responses have become more important than the actual difficult moments that I have lived through. These creative responses have become essential coping mechanisms that daily save me from quitting life. Walking on the Beach in a Girdle and High Heeled Boots are stories, declarations, prayers, exhales, poems that allow me to live a life open to possibilities in the midst of impossible-like life moments. Thank you for sharing in this journey with me. My hope is that you too will choose to respond creatively to live gallantly through every impossible situation and maybe even... WALK ON THE BEACH IN A GIRDLE AND HIGH HEELED BOOTS.

Day 1

Day 1

CLIMBING

My morning jog was filled with some challenging hills. As I fought to maintain my rhythm and breathing, I wondered, when was the incline going to break? GEESH! Hill after hill, I pondered the same thoughts and hill after hill I always met a level plain at the tip top of the hill that led to a beautiful descension. SHWHEW, now I'm able to catch my breath.

LESSON

Embrace the steep hills in your life. As you climb, breathe; inhaling and exhaling as you move forward and upward. Maintain a rhythm and pace that works for you, pausing often to catch your breath and rest. Remind yourself often; Things will level off right at the climax of your climb.

SCRIPTURE

Psalm 18:33 New English Translation (NET)

He gives me the agility of a deer; he enables me to negotiate the rugged terrain.

Psalm 23:1~2 The Passion Translation (TPT)

The Lord is my best friend and my shepherd. I always have more than enough. He offers a resting place for me in his luxurious love. His tracks take me to an oasis of peace, the quiet brook of bliss. That's where he restores and revives my life.

PRAYER

God, You are my strength and my shield. You cause me to rest in green pastures. You give me feet like hind's feet to climb upon high places. El Roi, you see me as I climb the rough and rugged paths. You, El Shaddai, restore my soul, laying me bedside green pastures as I walk by faith. Abba, You make every crooked place straight. Every high place is brought down in Jesus' name, Amen.

Day 2

Day 2

INTERLUDE - EXHALE - APPLICATION

I remember stepping off an airplane one Saturday morning thinking, it's got to be more to life than this. I felt like I was drowning in my children's successes and their failures while simultaneously being yanked by my husband's never-ending schedule; I couldn't think of not one thing that I had succeeded in or failed in for myself in a long while. Every high was based on their highs, every low based on their lows. The remainder of that day, I spent attempting to find me in the decisions I made and the things that I liked or disliked. I remember, I used to be "that girl" that loved to be immersed in just "LIVING" and living life without any fears or doubt. Where was she? Had she been killed, or did she simply die?

I suddenly realized that I still had a pulse but was not living. I remember looking back in time over my short life that had been filled with enough to fill two lifetimes, I discovered the tragedy that my memory brought forth mostly visuals of a lifeless body moving but missing moments to let life live me.

This was one of the lowest points in my life; I felt like I no longer wanted to exist. I didn't want to die but I just wanted to stop feeling. I didn't want to feel happy or sad as I didn't believe I could make it through the transition from one emotion to the other. I thought if

I just ceased being touched or affected by living, then I could walk through life a little better.

I began asking myself "Was my life "worth" the effort and energy to survive "through" all these valleys AND mountains?"

"What was so valuable about it; about me that I needed to or even desired to LIVE through all of these moments?"

"I thought that when you lived, you had life and life was supposed to be more interactive, enjoyable and embracing?"

"What inside of me was so valuable that all of this pressure was so necessary for my living life to be developed and pressured out?"

"Why continue paying for something that was gonna cost me more than just my existence, but my 'living life'?'

Living life had become a bit overrated.

Some of my Brokenness is still here. I have realized the difficulty of being broken and not allowing yourself to feel the pain…being numb to it all. I'm still peeling back to get to it to heal. As I peel back, I'm finding colors that I've never seen before…rainbows that have been born out of the rain and storms. My mental script is evolving… it's the way I think about myself …I now remember how important I am…I now remember how valuable I am. I want to remind you in this moment that you are valuable, you are important, and you are necessary.

I remember my decision that day. I decided, today I will begin to peel back the suffocating layers. Boy, what a day that was, filled with guilt and regret, while being surrounded by things that at one time brought me happiness and balance; somehow, now, it just didn't feel the same. I began to ask myself, am I doing this for "them" to prove a point that I really am a real person whose only name isn't "Mommy can I have?" or for me to deliver myself from suffocation and heal from self-neglect? I decided that, YES, this is for me...I think.

The Journey began that day by beginning to peel back the suffocating layers that I had allowed to redefine Jametta's original, specific purpose in life. Every day and even still today, I intentionally challenge myself to visualize doing the things that bring me happiness and align me with my purpose. I now ask myself what it feels like when I am doing those things. My response is to do those things. I now ride my bike every chance I get to embrace joy, contentment and most of all, it just makes me HAPPY! I desire to be free to feel; desire to be free to heal. Whom the son has set free is free indeed.

What will you do to intentionally challenge yourself to embrace joy, contentment and doing the things that make you happy?

List 3 Things

1. _____

2. _____

3. _____

SCRIPTURE

Psalm 139:16-18 The Passion Translation (TPT)

You saw who you created me to be before I became me! Before I'd ever seen the light of day, the number of days you planned for me were already recorded in your book. Every single moment you are thinking of me! How precious and wonderful to consider that you cherish me constantly in your every thought! O God, your desires toward me are more than the grains of sand on every shore! When I awake each morning, you're still with me.

PRAYER

God, my life belongs to you. Even when I am unaware of my purpose and worth, I am reminded you know the number of days you have planned for me. I am known by you despite what I don't know, YOU KNOW ME. Thank you Abba.

God is the source and strength of my life forever. May I always be aligned with your purpose for my life. As I move and matriculate daily in the world, may I always remember before I was formed in my mother's womb, you already knew me; you already knew the way that I take. Jireh, as I offer myself daily to your service through serving others whether they be family, friends, or colleagues, may the reason I do it be for Your glory. Amen.

Day 3

Day 3

DECLARATIONS

SAY IT OUT LOUD !

Today, I choose to influence.

Today, I am an influencer.

Today, I choose to intentionally be influenced by God's word and His will.

Today, everything I do, every breath I take, every task I engage will be from my unique special space and place in God.

CALL TO ACTION

How am I able to shine my light for Jesus today?

List 3 Ways

1. _____

2. _____

3. _____

SCRIPTURE

Matthew 5:14-16 -The Message Bible

Here's another way to put it: You're here to be light, bringing out the God-colors in the world. God is not a secret to be kept. We're going public with this, as public as a city on a hill. If I make you light-bearers, you don't think I'm going to hide you under a bucket, do you? I'm putting you on a light stand. Now that I've put you there on a hilltop, on a light stand—shine! Keep open house; be generous with your lives. By opening up to others, you'll prompt people to open up with God, this generous Father in heaven.

PRAYER

My life belongs to you God. May my light so shine that people will see your good works and glorify you. El Shaddai, may I be a living epistle daily, read by individuals I share space with. May the words of my mouth and the meditation of my heart be acceptable in your sight, my God and redeemer. May I seize every opportunity afforded to me to influence the world in a way that points back to you. Amen.

Day 4

Day 4

RENEW YOUR SQUEAL

While flying back from the DMV (Washington, Maryland, Virginia) on one occasion, I was enlightened by a 4-year-old sitting across the aisle who accompanied his grandmother on the plane. Oh, how he squealed peering out of the tiny window of the aircraft at the sight of the airplane take its wings and fly. His squeal shoved back in my soul the pure delight of what I've chunked as "normal"; the amazing feat for a couple of tons of steel to lift itself off the ground and soar suspended in the sky without anything holding it up. Some moments in life, we become so blinded by the "normality" of life that we miss precious, life moments where we embrace the sense of wonder for life.

LESSON

Be aware of everyday miracles:

- The formation of the erected stand of a bowed down plant once it receives water
- The setting of the sun at the end of the day
- The beautiful sound of raindrops during a heavy rainfall

Remember to harness the intrigue of the simplicity of everyday wonders all around us.

SCRIPTURE

Psalm 8:3, 9 The Passion Translation (TPT)

"Look at the splendor of your skies, your creative genius glowing in the heavens. When I gaze at your moon and your stars, mounted like jewels in their settings, I know you are the fascinating artist who fashioned it all! But I have to ask this question:"

"Yahweh, our Sovereign God, your glory streams from the heavens above, filling the earth with the majesty of your name! People everywhere see your splendor!"

PRAYER

Lord, my desire is to be aware of everyday miracles in my life. I have eyes to see and ears to here what you are speaking to me through people, places and things in your universe. I will never lose my wonder of all that you have created for my good and for the beauty of your holiness. You are Elohim, my Creator. Thank you, Lord.

Day 5

Day 5

As my sister from another mother sat at the Amtrak station with her grandchildren waiting for their train to take them to their Orlando Adventure, she face-timed me. Their train was scheduled for a 9:15am departure, but as they checked in, they learned their train was delayed for 2 hours with a new departure time of 11:15am. I suddenly felt a knot in my tummy as concern quickly overshadowed my joy: That gut punch feeling of a kid having to wait longer than the appointed time they were initially promised. These thoughts erupted out in my head, "How are the kids handling this delay? Did they faint? Did they fall on the floor kicking and screaming because their time with Mickey and Minnie was delayed? Are they nagging you, asking, begging, crying 'Are we gonna leave yet?' While in that tsunami of thoughts, my friend turned the phone camera around. To my astonishment, the camera shared a visual of these two kids outside of the train station's waiting area, DANCING to music that wasn't playing. They were grinning as if they were already at Mickey and Minnie's house dancing to "It's a Small World After All". I yelled into the phone to her, "What's wrong with those kids? They are acting as if they are already at their destination, and they haven't even left yet!"

LESSON

Intentionally embrace the posture of a little child. Children only allow stuff to bother them for a moment and then they forget about it because they know that they have some bigger people who have their back. They play effortlessly, living in the moment. They move forward in life, fearing nothing because they have been told they are going somewhere even when delayed. In the meantime, they dance until the delay of departure passes. Once on the way, they take in all the sites, seizing every opportunity to see what they can see on the way and do what they can do on the way. And when they get there, they play with no regrets and no thought of what it took for them to get there.

SCRIPTURE

2 Corinthians 4:15-18 J B Phillips

We wish you could see how all this is working out for your benefit, and how the more grace God gives, the more thanksgiving will redound to his glory. This is the reason why we never collapse. The outward man does indeed suffer wear and tear, but every day the inward man receives fresh strength. These little troubles (which are really so transitory) are winning for us a permanent, glorious and solid reward out of all proportion to our pain. For we are looking all the time not at the visible things but at the invisible. The visible things are transitory: it is the invisible things that are really permanent.

PRAYER

El Olam, Everlasting Father, my life is in your hands. even in the midst of delays, disappointments, and catastrophe, I yet trust you. I will wait on you. You never leave me nor forsake me. You go before me making every crooked place straight, bringing every high place down, in Jesus' name. Amen.

Day 6

Day 6

DECLARATIONS

Today, I choose the wind as my transporter.

Today, I choose positive, life-giving words as my nourishment.

Today, I choose peace as my cloak.

Today, I choose to intentionally throw off hindrances and blockages that sideline my productivity.

Today, I choose gratitude over anxiety.

Today, I choose to embrace the strength that joy brings over the suffocation of bitterness.

Today, I will intentionally ride the wind, with no concern of where it may carry me.

Today, while settled in on my unique journey and path, I will trust my steps and the transporter, God.

SCRIPTURE

Isaiah 46:4-6 The Voice

And when you are old, I will still be there, carrying you. When your limbs grow tired, your eyes are weak, And your hair a silvery gray, I will carry you as I always have. I will carry you and save you. Does anyone compare to Me? Can you find any likeness? Who or what might be My equal or even close to Me?

PRAYER

God, I am because you are. You create intended paths for me to journey even when I'm not sure where I'll end up. I trust your guidance and direction every day of my life. My life belongs to you. Wherever you lead me, I will follow; I'll go with You all the way. My confidence is in you El Roi, my God who sees me. Amen.

Day 7

Day 7

If any of you have ever authentically experienced a "check out" moment, you understand, like me, the sheer feeling of EVERYTHING being too much. To feel and be touched by the daily "check-ins" of life in some moments seem overrated. Some days, the overwhelming weight of the responsibility of living causes me to desire to "check out" of life; not die, just check out. Check out from the responsibility of health and wealth; check out from the responsibility of parenting and partnering; check out from the mere expectation of arising and maneuvering as a sane and sound human being.

LESSON

Learn to just stop, for a moment; for 2 minutes or 10 minutes; anything. STOP! DO NOTHING. NOT ONE THING. Just be. Stop, allow yourself to be replenished by the tasks of nothingness of just being; a space where nothing else matters except your be-ING.

SCRIPTURE

Psalm 91:1 The Passion Translation (TPT)

When you abide under the shadow of Shaddai, you are hidden in the strength of God Most High.

Colossians 3:15 New International Version (NIV)

And let the peace of Christ rule in your hearts, to which indeed you called one body. And be thankful.

Psalm 61:2 The Passion Translation (TPT)

For no matter where I am, even when I'm far from home, I will cry out to you for a father's help. When I'm feeble and overwhelmed by life, guide me into your glory, where I am safe and sheltered.

PRAYER

Abba, when my heart is overwhelmed, lead me to the rock that is higher than I. Allow me to remember the strength of your hand. May I always rest in the confidence of your grace being sufficient for me even in my weakness. Forever, my life is in your hands. Amen.

Day 8

Day 8

INTERLUDE – EXHALE - APPLICATION

Create Your Own Music

Make a decision to disown other people's challenges and proclivities that suck all the life out of you. Give it back to them and create a path and process to journey through YOUR life, dancing to YOUR own beat, YOUR own music, even if it IS unique.

Embrace being preoccupied with creating your own music, writing your own song, dancing to your own beat. You will find that it will become more difficult to be distracted and deterred by someone else's choice of music (decisions) and song (consequences). Be intentional in your focus while utilizing your energy to create your own music and writing your own lyrics for your life's journey.

Write out your own music today. Simply jot down 3 things you are able to identify to do today which line up with your purpose.

1. _____

2. _____

3. _____

SCRIPTURE

Jeremiah 1:5 The Living Bible

"I knew you before you were formed within your mother's womb; before you were born I sanctified you and appointed you as my spokesman to the world."

PRAYER

Elohim, my God who knew before I was created in my mother's womb. You are my everything. All that I am is because of you. Every assignment attached to my life you already know. Every space and place I was created for, you've already prepared. May I be intentional in my focus on the things that are for me, for my voice, for my hands, for my intellectual property. I trust you to lead and guide me every step of the way. Amen.

Day 9

Day 9

My cloth is different, tattered, but strong. I will always be great at being who I know I am and should be. I will listen to my inside voice, Holy Spirit, clear the noise, buckle back into what I have always known that keeps me anchored in Yahweh's presence. My posture will determine the flow and depth of rivers in my private time with God. I am valuable and necessary for then, now and for the rest of my life. I AM AN INFLUENCER. I have a voice - I WILL USE IT!

Today, I choose to listen to my inside voice.

Today, I choose to clear the noise.

Today, I choose to flow with God in His presence.

Today, I am valuable.

SCRIPTURE

Jeremiah 29:11 The Message Bible

I know what I'm doing. I have it all planned out—plans to take care of you, not abandon you, plans to give you the future you hope for.

John 16:13 New Living Translation (NLT)

When the Spirit of truth comes, he will guide you into all truth. He will not speak on his own but will tell you what he has heard. He will tell you about the future.

PRAYER

As I avail myself to you daily God, may I always be reminded that you are the potter - I am the clay. As you are my creator, Elohim, I will always desire You and Your presence as a place of safety, peace, instruction, and worship. May my voice today echo your voice in what I speak about myself and others. May my posture be reminiscent of one who has been with You, been in your presence open to receive you and your word. Holy Spirit, lead me and guide me into always in truth. Amen.

Day 10

Day 10

DANCING ON THE 'TATER CHIP AISLE

While in the grocery store one day, I saw a little girl who appeared to be 8 years old prancing; dancing, gliding wistfully with her dad. As she glided through the aisles, she was chattering aloud to her dad; and to anyone, it seemed, in close proximity. Then, suddenly, I heard and saw a big ole PLOP in the middle of the potato chip aisle. The little girl glider had fallen flat onto the floor in mid glide. While on the floor, out of her mouth erupts a big ole ball of laughter. Meanwhile, her dad moved swiftly to peer over this pile of human laughter. As she was rebounding, her dad carefully inquired, "What happened?" She said "I fell because I'm tired. He said, "Sure doesn't look like it!"

While all of this was happening, I was standing by at the end of the tater chip aisle, literally laughing out loud while crying all at the same time. After I left the store, I was energized to push up and out. I was empowered to speak life and live in light. Why should I choice to muddle? Go ahead, jump up and start dancing again.

LESSON

1. Embrace life like a child. Do unexpected things in unexpected

places. Dance in the grocery store on the tater chip aisle while everyone's watching. Express yourself authentically daily in your environment. If the spaces you occupy refuse to accommodate you, change the rules or change your environment.

2. Be honest and in tune with yourself about all of you and your capacity. The little girl keenly understood the culprit for her weakness, the cause of her fall. She IMMEDIATELY identified, recognized and confessed the culprit..."I'm tired!". She wasn't ashamed or dismayed; it was a fact, it was truth. "I fell because I was tired." IT IS WHAT IT IS! No hiding or ducking. No excuses or muddling.

3. Get up. The little girl glider immediately picked herself up WHILE laughing. She didn't take herself that seriously. It wasn't the end of the world. She didn't stay in that same place, become contorted, paralyzed, retarded, or congested. She fell and she got back up. After she got up, she didn't allow the environment to cause her to change who she was. She got up frolicking again! Remind yourself often, THIS TOO SHALL PASS. Little girl glider was again up dancing down the 'tater chip aisle.

SCRIPTURE

2 Corinthians 4:8-12 Contemporary English Version (CEV)

We often suffer, but we are never crushed. Even when we don't know what to do, we never give up. In times of trouble, God is with us, and when we are knocked down, we get up again. We face death every day because of Jesus. Our bodies show what his death was like, so that his life can also be seen in us. This means that death is working in us, but life is working in you.

PRAYER

Oh my God, my help. You are all wise. There is none that compares to your "IS"NESS. The heavens declare your glory. My earthen vessel quakes at your sovereignty. Thank you for being in the midst of us. We are not moved by the ways of this world. we will never give up as long as you are with us. Your word says you will never leave us nor forsake us. be all glory, power and dominion forever. Amen.

Day 11

Day 11

For us.

We who desire to.

Survive.

Thrive.

Live Alive.

We must.

We have to.

Keep.

Getting.

Up.

Only after.

We take.

Time.

To.

Be healed.

CALL TO ACTION

Take a moment. Inhale. Exhale. Breathe. Now, think about 3 things, whether emotional or physical, you need to be healed and made whole from.

1. _____

2. _____

3. _____

SCRIPTURE

Malachi 4:2 New English Translation (NET)

But for you who respect my name, the sun of vindication will rise with healing wings, and you will skip about like calves released from the stall.

John 11:40 New Living Translation (NLT)

Jesus responded, "Didn't I tell you that you would see God's glory if you believe?"

PRAYER

Jehovah Rapha, my healer, thank you for your healing virtue that daily I have access to. We agree with you for miracles signs and wonders to heal all manner of disease. We stand on your word by faith, that whatever we ask in your name, we have. Our lives are livings examples of what you can do with one who believes. We trust your name, we are confident that at your name Jesus, every knee of discomfort, mentally, physically and spiritually shall bow. Amen.

Day 12

Day 12

REFUSE THE ROLLERCOASTER

Amusements parks are one of my favorite places to go. Every ride in the park is my delight, especially the MONSTER ROLLER COASTERS!

I love the extreme thrill of the anticipation of what seems to be a never-ending moment of fear, excitement, nervousness and sheer CRAZINESS all at the same time! The ascent of the coaster pushes my stomach to my throat while the descent of the coaster takes my heart to my feet; every jerk of the curves is filled with delightful shrieks and uncontrolled laughter, all in a matter of seconds.

Now when it comes to riding a roller coaster outside of an amusement park, I am more inclined, now, to REFUSE THE ROLLER COASTER. Riding a rollercoaster outside of an amusement park can be fatal to the health of one's stability; opening the potential to unsettle a good life rhythm. When you ride a roller coaster outside of an amusement park, you give permission to persons to take you on traumatizing and unhealthy emotional and mental rides. You find yourself on a steep emotional ascent, while climbing; filled with thrill, excitement, and anticipation only to be dropped by a quick descent or a sharp unanticipated curve that leaves you wondering what just happened while your heart is broken and your mind shattered.

LESSON

All of us have choices on this journey and one of the greatest choices that we have is to choose to live a life that is free of allowing persons permission to disrupt and unsettle our lives by their selfish and insensitive behaviors. One of the ways we can live our lives ANCHORED is to give ourselves permission to REFUSE THE ROLLER COASTER.

Choose every day to get out of line for that fatal roller coaster. Why wait in a long line for something that is going to cause you more damage than good? If you are already on the coaster, unfasten your seatbelt and simply get off...ITS NOT TOO LATE!!!

SCRIPTURE

Philippians 4:6-9 The Passion Translation (TPT)

"Don't be pulled in different directions or worried about a thing. Be saturated in prayer throughout each day, offering your faith-filled requests before God with overflowing gratitude. Tell him every detail of your life, then God's wonderful peace that transcends human understanding, will guard your heart and mind through Jesus Christ. Keep your thoughts continually fixed on all that is authentic and real, honorable and admirable, beautiful and respectful, pure and holy, merciful and kind. And fasten your thoughts on every glorious work of God, praising him always. Put into practice the example of all that you have heard from me or seen in my life and the God of peace will be with you in all things."

PRAYER

God, our hope is always in you. We rest is your word as we daily walk in the earth. May we always be clear and aware to choose what is right and purposeful for my life. May I be open to hear you speak throughout the day to inhabit spaces and places with people I have been assigned to. Thank you for holy boldness to choose what complements your will for my life. In Jesus' name, Amen.

Day 13

Day 13

We are still here family. Despite every situation; Despite every disappointment; We are still here. Despite the pressure, pain and near-death experiences; We are still here. Despite our own sabotage; Despite the deliberate attacks; Despite the nights of praying and crying; We are still here. No matter what you are experiencing today, WE ARE STILL HERE! Grab a hold of this day and make it the best day of your life. God has kept you to demonstrate His ability to keep you when nothing or no one else can...remind yourself...I AM STILL HERE!

Today, I choose a life free and clear of unhealthy influences.

Today I choose to recognize choices on this journey.

Today I choose to make today a day free from allowing others permission to disrupt and unsettle my life by selfish and insensitive behaviors.

Today, I choose to give myself permission to refuse opportunities where any individual or circumstance displaces me from my intended journey.

Today, I choose to abandon spaces that suffocate and deflate.

Today, I choose to inhabit spaces that increase and uplift.

Today, I choose to live free and clear to be who I BE.

SCRIPTURE

Isaiah 43:2 New Living Translation (NLT)

"When you go through deep waters, I will be with you. When you go through rivers of difficulty, you will not drown. When you walk through the fire of oppression, you will not be burned up; the flames will not consume you."

PRAYER

I pray today for your strength; I pray today for your might; I pray today for peace in your mind in the midst of every contrary circumstance. I pray today for your understanding so that you will recognize the hand of God in your life. I pray today for your present; that you will stay focused on your prophetic destiny so that what you see today will not distract you from what God has ALREAY prepared for you. I pray for your hunger; that you will seek God to satisfy you instead of seeking ungodly satisfaction. I declare and decree that God will be God today and every day in your life, your Savior and Lord.

Day 14

Day 14

I witnessed a kid in the parking lot running around a vehicle playing with abandonment with no care or pretense. Oh the wonder of transforming a familiar object into a place and space, wherever I am of play and joy. I'm wondering if I embraced the mindset of a child, remembering to play and run every chance I get. Never taking life so serious that I miss moments to run and play even while surrounded by familiar people and things. I don't have to wait until I have play clothes on to play. I don't have to wait until I get off work or vacation. Daily I am able to engage in fun and activities. I don't have to even wait until I have a partner, I am able to create a playground any and everywhere I go and am. I am reminding myself that I am a playground.

CALL TO ACTION

You get to create a life that you desire and deserve. You get to live daily in freedom and adventure. What will you do this week to create moments of adventure infused in your daily routine?

1. _____

2. _____

3. _____

SCRIPTURE

John 10:9-10 American Standard Version (ASV)

Anyone who goes through me will be cared for—will freely go in and out, and find pasture. A thief is only there to steal and kill and destroy. I came so they can have real and eternal life, more and better life than they ever dreamed of.

PRAYER

Jehovah, my God, my redeemer, my prince of peace, my light, thank you for joy unspeakable, full of glory. Daily you load us with the benefit of your presence, your peace, your kindness, your love. Daily you capture us with your word that meets us where we are. God, we never desire to ever lose our wonder of who you are and what we have access to. We will forever trust you, your love and your presence. Amen.

Epilogue

Heaven is an unrivaled irrigation system that supplies rain and snow to the earth to provide necessary nutrients and moisture for growth. The result is growth and maturity for all plant and animal life in the earth. I get the picture...that big ole pine tree towering over everything in my parents' yard has gulped lots of moisture, more rain than snow, to command the center stage of the yard. Its growth is the result of the right type of nutrients feeding and watering it...Papa Pine had no other choice but to grow due to it being watered and fed.

Isaiah 55:10~11 pricks my heart and spirit. How many times, just yesterday, did I poison my potential with my negative thoughts that manifested to nouns, pronouns, adjectives, and verbs that have the ability to influence the direction of my today, tomorrow and my future. Mann, every noun, pronoun, adjective, and verb that comes out of my mouth are forming and creating my world. TEARS!

Isaiah 55:10~11 (NET)

> [10] *The rain and snow fall from the sky*
> *and do not return,*
> *but instead water the earth*
> *and make it produce and yield crops,*
> *and provide seed for the planter and food for those who must eat.*
> [11] *In the same way, the promise that I make*

does not return to me, having accomplished nothing.
No, it is realized as I desire
and is fulfilled as I intend.

In my distress and anxiety, what have I been feeding and nourishing my potential...deadly poison or rich nutrients? At the end of the day, nerves frayed and body exhausted, how am I framing my tomorrow? In my daily conversations, is my speech betraying my faith and tearing down my promises? How many times have I, myself, worked against myself by the fragmented building blocks that I created with my own damning words?

(SCREAMIMG!) LORD, allow the words of my mouth and the meditation of my heart to be acceptable in thy sight oh Lord my strength and redeemer! God please help me to be so consumed with whatever is true, whatever is honorable, whatever is just, whatever is pure, whatever is lovely, whatever is commendable, if there is any excellence, if there is anything worthy of praise. God hear my heart, enter onto my path, inhabit my thoughts, stream through in my speech, influence my thoughts...LEAD ME, GUIDE ME OH GREAT JEHOVAH!

Resources

Holy Bible, American Standard Version (ASV)

Holy Bible, J. B. Phillips New Testament

Holy Bible, The Living Bible (TLB)

Holy Bible, The Message Bible (MSG)

Holy Bible, New English Translation (NET)

Holy Bible, New International Version (NIV)

Holy Bible, New Living Translation (NLT)

Holy Bible, The Passion Translation (TPT)

Holy Bible, The Voice

About The Author

J ANN

Jametta Chandler Moore, affectionately known as J Ann, is a multilayered woman of business and faith. She is an Author, Minister, Speaker, Facilitator and Entrepreneur. Through these facets, she is able to share space with individuals from all walks of life. J Ann's most powerful tool of connection is transparency which allows her to educate, empower and provoke individuals with compassion. J Ann champions the world through Life Anchor Enterprises LLC. Life Anchor Enterprises LLC is an umbrella that houses several initiatives that seek to empower, educate, and provoke individuals to identify and embrace their God-given potential and purpose.

J Ann resides in Charleston, South Carolina. Her sense of adventure and desire to impact individuals, compels her to expand her reach through travel all throughout these United States and all over the world.

Fun Facts:

Loves to cartwheel wherever, whenever

Drove school bus while in high school

Did missions and evangelized in East Africa

"Every day you are alive is an adventure."

CPSIA information can be obtained
at www.ICGtesting.com
Printed in the USA
LVHW082022080822
725450LV00013B/447